BENNY BANDAGE

BENNY BANDAGE

by BARBARA KIDDER

Publishers T. S. DENISON & COMPANY, INC. *Minneapolis, Minnesota*

T. S. DENISON & COMPANY, INC.

First Printing—January 1968
Second Printing—April 1969
Third Printing—August 1971

Standard Book Number: 513-00299-5
Library of Congress Card Number: 67-28675
Printed in the United States of America
by The Brings Press
Copyright © MCMLXVII by T. S. Denison & Co., Inc.
Minneapolis, Minn. 55437

ACKNOWLEDGMENT

We wish to thank Miss Lula Neuman, chairman of the Safety Committee for the North Dakota State Health Curriculum, for prepublication reviewal of Benny Bandage.

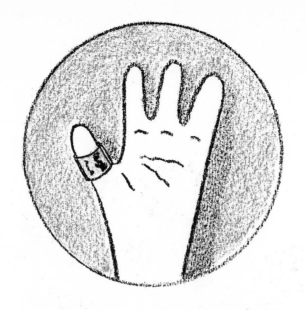

BENNY BANDAGE

Rusty was carving a model airplane from a block of wood. He was going to give it to Dad for his birthday. The knife slipped and cut Rusty's thumb. He ran upstairs to Mother who cleaned his thumb and put a bandage over the cut to keep the dirt out.

Rosie was roller-skating on the sidewalk in front of her house. The sun was shining and it was warm and pleasant. She looked up at a robin which was singing in the elm tree. Rosie did not see the big crack in the sidewalk so she tripped and fell. Mother washed Rosie's skinned knee and put a bandage on it to keep it clean.

Benny Bandage is our good friend. He helps us when we get a small injury, like a cut or scrape. But there are some hurts which are too big for Benny to handle. He wants to tell you a story about safety so that you will know how to keep away from dangerous things which might injure you.

Benny says, "If you make it a habit to learn safety, most accidents won't happen. You can have more fun if you plan to be safe.

"No one causes an accident on purpose, but some do so because they are careless."

Some people want to do as they please. They do not care if their actions are a danger to those about them. Rusty is shooting arrows at a tree across the street. Do you see an accident that could happen?

Some people are daydreamers and do not pay attention to what they are doing. Rosie is reading a book as she crosses the street. Do you see an accident that could happen?

Some people get excited easily and rush to do something without thinking. Rosie is running after her ball which bounced into the street. Do you see an accident that could happen?

Some people are show-offs who take dangerous chances. Rusty is showing off on his bicycle. Do you see an accident that could happen?

HOME SAFETY

Benny says, "We often feel the safest at home. But death and injuries can happen more often at home than any other place."

Falls cause many injuries. Find the danger in each picture.

FIRES and BURNS can be prevented.

Do not leave piles of paper or rubbish about.

Clean your closet of old clothes and broken things.

Every smoker should have an ash tray.

Good housekeeping makes safer living.

Do not play
with matches.

Do not handle anything
electrical with wet hands.

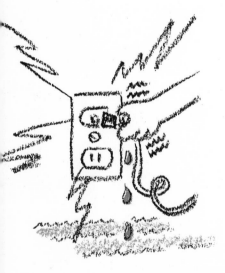

If there is a fire in
your house, leave by a
door or window far-
thest from the fire. Do
not try to save any
belongings.

There are POISONS in the house you should stay away from.

Some medicines are poisonous if not used right.

Alcohol should be kept out of reach.

Spray cans can be dangerous.

Cleaning fluids can give off dangerous fumes.

Bleaches, drain cleaners, and cosmetics can be dangerous.

DANGEROUS OBJECTS should be left alone.

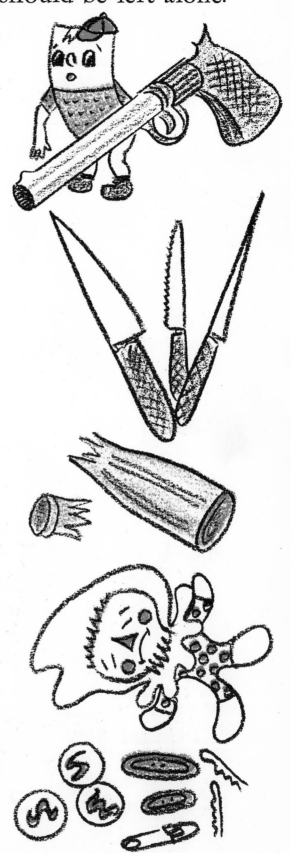

Father's gun could be loaded. Do not play with it.

Mother's knives are sharp. Do not play with them.

Glass objects can be broken. Do not try to pick up broken pieces of glass. Mother or Father will help you.

Plastic bags are air-tight. Do not put them over anyone's head. He could not breathe.

Small objects could be swallowed. Do not put them into your mouth. A sudden cough or sneeze could make them go down the wrong way and cause you to choke.

There are DANGEROUS AREAS
to stay away from.

Excavations and construction

Dump yards

Open wells

Water areas and ice

Strange dogs should be left alone. They might not trust you and may bite to protect themselves.

Bicycle riding can be fun, but ride safely and follow good driving rules on the street. When you get your license get a list of rules, too, and read them.

SCHOOL SAFETY

Benny says, "School safety is important too." When you **cross streets** going to and from school, be alert.

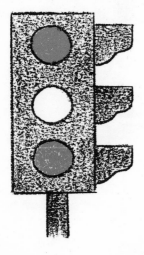

Where there is a signal, stop on the yellow and red lights, go on the green.

Where there is no signal, look both to the left and to the right before you cross. Watch for cars that may be turning.

Where there is a school patrol, mind his signals and go when he tells you to.

Do not accept **rides from strangers.** It is better to walk than not get there at all.

If you **ride a bus,** do not push and shove to get on. Do not run in front of the bus when you get off.

While you are **in school** do not run or push.

On the playground, follow the rules and be a good sport. Be thoughtful when you play on school ground equipment and wait for your turn.

Be considerate when you go back into the school. Remember, you are not only protecting yourself, but you are protecting the safety of others.

There are **other dangers.** Benny cannot tell you all of the dangers there are, but he would like to keep you from getting hurt.

On these two pages find these dangers: Burning leaves or trash. Firecrackers. Sand or snow tunnels. Old refrigerator. Climbing trees too high. Climbing steep banks or cliffs.

Benny says,
"Be smart.
Live safely.
Keep happy."